Letters to a Young Priest

Letters to a Young Priest
from a laicised priest

Anton Grabner-Haider

Veritas Publications Dublin 1975

First published 1975 by
Veritas Publications,
Pranstown House, Booterstown Avenue,
Co. Dublin.

An einen jungen Priester
Published originally in German
by Veritas-Verlag, Wien-Linz-Passau.

Printed and bound in the Republic of Ireland
at The Dolmen Press, Dublin.

Designed by Liam Miller.

ISBN 0-901810-88-6
Cat. No. 3315

Contents

Letter 1   Problems of the Faith   9

Letter 2   Spirituality   21

Letter 3   A Living Sign   33

Letter 4   Celibacy   43

Letter 5   Dialogue and Criticism   53

We greatly need you to live your particular form of life; it accompanies the word you preach and, indeed, prepares the way for it. We need that word, for it has power to change men, to change the world. We all need to be strengthened in faith. I would be happy to think that through this correspondence I had contributed a little towards strengthening you in your vocation.

Letter 1
Problems of the Faith

For myself I have no alternative but to believe in God because I have experienced his grace and his power in my life.

My dear brother,

Permit me to address you in this way, for until recently I was one of your brother-priests. You may be surprised to receive a letter from me but the fact is that, since I left, I have been thinking a lot about the priesthood. Indeed, my thoughts keep continually returning to it; that is not to be wondered at, since it was my vocation; sometimes I think it has remained my vocation. I have not always felt like this, but my thinking on the priest-hood seems to have developed, so much so that I want to share my thoughts on the subject with you.

You begin your work as a priest in a difficult time. As you know, many people nowadays ask, "What do we need priests for?" This question comes not only from those outside the Church but also from those within; it is raised by priests and laymen alike. They hold that by virtue of Baptism all the baptised are priests and that therefore the Church has no need of a priestly caste. This opinion seems to have been arrived at without much reflection. Those who advance it probably know Scripture, but I wonder are they taking the whole Bible, the whole New Testament, into con-sideration? I cannot help wondering, too, how extensive, how deep is their knowledge of human life and society. The opinions they express, the questions they ask must make it difficult for you as you begin your priestly life.

I have a great deal of respect for your decision, your commitment, which you undertook knowing that you face difficulties. Today, the priesthood is not popular; it is not considered a "trendy" calling. Your decision was your own, supported no doubt by the prayers of many of the faithful. I see this decision of yours as something that frees you from certain pressures. You have shown, and in a very effective way, that you do not have to conform, to be "in the swim" to be happy; indeed, you have shown that happiness is to be found elsewhere. That gladdens my heart. Certainly the situation has grown more difficult than it was ten years ago when I made a similar decision.

I often ask myself why life has become so hard for priests today, and I have given much thought to my reasons for revoking my decision. Later on I will tell you what I have and what I have not revoked. I will tell you of the difficulties that troubled me then, difficulties that I now see in a different light. To give you some insight into these problems, I must first describe how things were in my time.

Like many others, I began the study of theology in a revolutionary period. John XXIII was Pope and had summoned a Pastoral Council. Biblical thinking was beginning to make itself felt in theology. We read the Bible, making discoveries in it that filled us with enthusiasm. It was a liberating mode of thought and, for us, a liberating faith. We felt that we were close to the origins of the Church and of Christian existence, and wanted to communicate these discoveries to the Church of our time. We discovered many forgotten dimensions of faith, and also of prayer. Our common search for the footprints of Jesus in the Bible gave us a strong sense of community.

At the same time we were seeking the original forms of worship and liturgy. We delighted in experimenting with these forms which we hoped would be welcomed with new understanding by modern man. We hoped that this would revolutionise pastoral care. The Council itself encouraged us when it gave pride of place to the liturgy in its first session. We used biblical thought-forms to create our worship. We sang biblical chants and hymns. We had discovered a new dimension of faith.

I must admit that this made us proud. Some of us became arrogant, looking down on traditional neoscholastic theology and pitying those who taught it. We adopted a "kneeling theology", striving for a strong spirituality to sustain us. We discovered not only the Bible but also the writings of saints like Thérèse of Lisieux, Teresa of Avila and John of the Cross and of Christians who had wrestled for faith—Péguy, Bloy, Claudel, Teilhard de Chardin, Le Fort and others. The experiment of the Worker Priests fascinated us. We dreamed of a new language for the faith, a language intelligible to our contemporaries.

We longed for a more detailed, a more accurate knowledge of Scripture, so exegesis, the historico-critical examination of the sacred texts, became our master. Some of us attended university faculties where particularly eminent professors of exegesis were to be found. Protestant scholars held us spellbound and that at a time when the ecumenical movement was gathering strength. Slowly, imperceptibly, our original "kneeling theology" gave place to a "sitting theology". As we did not notice this change, neither did we notice in what direction the sitting theology was tending; a subtle fallacy lay concealed in it which contributed much to the ensuing insecurity.

We failed to notice that this theology was forever looking over its shoulder at modern knowledge — as though it felt itself threatened, pursued by the achievements of the exact sciences, as though it felt obliged to vie with them. For that reason it adopted a learned tone, chased eagerly after every new theory and was continually trying to be in the lead. I am not referring to official Church theology, the kind of theology that was prepared to give an account of its relationship with the tradition of the faith. I refer rather to a theology which was not prepared to justify itself in that forum, preferring to hawk its wares through a superficially intellectual Vanity Fair. Several of us were deluded by it, since we hoped to find in it a new language for the Gospel.

We used to deplore that the Gospel language, which brought so much joy to us, was not understood by many of our contemporaries. For this we blamed either antiquated theology or existing practices. We searched passionately for a new Gospel language. With that great witness for the faith, Bonhoeffer, we dreamed of a language which would again change the world, of a Church which would exist wholly for the sake of the world. That last phrase was written on many of our ordination cards. Our quest took us far afield, among writers, philosophers and the theologians we regarded as modern; by this time we had more or less forsaken the saints.

A number of simple solutions were offered by this modern theology. The Gospel would have to be de-mythologised, then people would again understand its language. By getting rid of symbols, myths and miracle-terminology, we would be left with the core, the heart of the Gospel. An obsolete idea of God should be replaced by a new one. No one had a direct line to God, we were told; the only way to achieve encounter with God was through one's fellow human-beings; the cultivation of personal relationships with God should be abandoned. As for the increasing secularisation of society, we should not try to resist its progress; on the contrary its development should be encouraged, that being the only way to acquire a "pure" faith. Christianity was not a "religion", since we could only speak of God in secular terms. If we did all this we were assured that people would once more understand the Gospel.

It was only too easy for a man who had difficulties of faith to get "hooked" on these superficialities. Young priests and theologians were particularly vulnerable to the lure of these supposedly new ways. If contrary arguments were heard at all they seemed very remote and we dismissed them as "not progressive". And so it happened that priests who, through a genuine desire for enlightenment, lent an ear to these solutions, began to flounder in great personal difficulties: If the faith has to be secularised, what is the point of consecrated personnel? If we can only speak to God in secular terms, what justification is there for spiritual signs, for clergy? If Christianity is not a religion, if Jesus was not himself a priest, if he did not intend that there should be priests, perhaps the priesthood is not legitimate at all? Perhaps the priest is actually hindering the Gospel?

You may imagine the deep inner conflicts suffered by many priests as a result of all this. They had responded to a divine call and wanted to continue to respond, when suddenly their chosen form of life was robbed of its justification. Above all, the fact that we had renounced marriage was somehow left in the air. It became necessary to seek a new form of life, even though that meant opposing the Church's wishes. We had to take back a promise made to the Church and to a concrete community. This we did with heavy hearts, but to many of us there seemed no other way out. I have been trying to show you the theological development that lay behind our conflicts and decisions, a development I since recognise to have been the result of an ideology, a theology gone astray.

Let me attempt to explain how I now see the grave errors involved. They may appear differently to you who regard them from a different viewpoint, but I would like to help you avoid such pitfalls. I see the theology to which I refer as disturbed in its relationship to contemporary knowledge. It has not sufficiently clarified the basic relationship between knowledge and faith, nor does it always make clear the uniqueness and the logical status of affirmations of faith. As Simone Weil observed, it has a "bad conscience" in the presence of modern science and it communicates this to the faithful. Insecure itself, it spreads insecurity.

I confess that I have shared that insecurity, and theology was unable to preserve me from it. Not until I began to look more closely at a contemporary theory of knowledge did I realise that the insecurity has no justification. The relationship between knowledge and faith can be determined exactly and shows an inner consistency. From the viewpoint of empirical science the question of God cannot be decided one way or another. The probability is fifty-fifty. That leaves me with perfect freedom to believe, just as it implies that others have the same freedom not to believe. For myself I have no alternative but to believe in God because I have experienced his grace and his power in my life. My faith has become free; it need not fear any rational argument.

16

Linguistic analysis and the theory of language were the means of introducing me to the unique, logical status of this faith. Faith is a personal relationship with God. God, however, is the transcendental object of religion. Therefore Christian faith, which is both a personal relationship with God and the expression of that relationship, is a religious faith.

Those theologians who are consumed with zeal for the secularising of God have produced no analysis of faith or of the language of faith. Nor are they able to do so. Specialists regard their approach as a misuse of the language of faith; it seems to me that what they are doing is changing the fundamental constitution of faith.

The same may be said of the de-mythologisers. They are unable to give any insight into the logical structure of the language of faith. That language has two dimensions, descriptive and non-descriptive. The latter is by far the more preponderant and cannot do without linguistic symbols and images. Through these symbols and images we relate to God in language, in linguistic acts of faith. The various solutions suggested for a new language of faith are no solutions at all. Logically they are inconsistent. They betray a maladjustment *vis-à-vis* modern knowledge; but there can be no doubt that they have played a decisive role in undermining the security of faith in the Church today.

What follows from this? That an exclusively

"horizontal" idea of God is not Christian; on the contrary God is religion's transcendental object, on the analogy of the human person. Our relation to him is therefore analogous to our relation to a human person. A vertical relation to God gives rise to a horizontal relation, not *vice versa*. God encounters man in a "disclosure" which contains empirical and other added elements. Man replies to this disclosure in linguistic acts of faith — wonder, thanksgiving, fear, joy — which we call prayer.

If you have followed me thus far, you will have realised that the importance of theology is relative. The linguistic expressions of faith come first; then, and only then, the secondary "talk" about this, the science of faith. I do not want to undermine your confidence in theology. I know that there is a theology which not only seeks for a new language to express faith, but also continually assesses its own compatibility with the faith in its entirety. But I *do* want to draw your attention to these points, so that you may become discriminating. The stakes are high.

I am sorry if what I have said sounds formal and theoretical, but I urge you to get the issues clear in your mind, especially in the modern situation. Only by doing so will you be able to look each argument calmly in the face; only then will you be inwardly free, able to proclaim the Gospel with a good conscience. The young Wittgenstein once said: "Even when all the problems of science are solved, we shall be no nearer solving the problems of our own lives." Whatever our knowledge, these problems (e.g. What is the meaning of life? How can I make a success of my life?) will remain. And today such problems appear to be even more pressing. There is a great thirst within us, a thirst for meaning, a thirst for faith.

Another thing: scientific knowledge is always provisional. By definition it is fallible and subject to revision. It always contains an element of hypothesis. Strange as it may seem to an age dependent on it, science can give us no ultimate security. We theologians need to remember that, prone as we are to over-estimate its results. Faith, on the contrary, is totally different. In its basic structure it is definitive, not subject to change. The relation of man to God is a constant.

In conclusion let me tell you what I think is possible, what I dream of. On the one hand we need exact, logical thought in theology, using the refined criteria of modern scholarship; on the other hand we must have a deep spirituality rooted in the faith. I believe that these two requirements can be found in one and the same person. I am afraid that the theology we learned made too many compromises; its spirituality became shallow and it neglected precision in its thought.

It seems to me that we need to maintain the tension between "sitting" and "kneeling" theology; that is the only way to avoid serious mistakes in our thinking. Furthermore, only in this tension can faith strike root again. For it looks as though the process of uprooting and undermining is well advanced; it will be your part and mine to help with the work of replanting.

Letter 2
Spirituality

A vocation is brought to fruition by being continually rooted in faith and by a constant deepening of one's spiritual life.

My dear friend,

I hope that you were not put off by my pre-
occupation with theoretical problems of the faith
in my last letter. These problems concern me a
great deal and I take it for granted that they
concern you too, to some extent. They urgently
need clearing up, for they can hinder those who
are trying to respond to the Gospel vocation. They
are not, of course, fundamental, the essential thing
is the call to serve the Church, the vocation to the
Gospel of Jesus.

The shape that this vocation takes is different
for each person. But in every case what happens
is basically the same and no one can completely
escape it. You can recall the time when you first
felt the desire to become a priest. You had a
particular idea of what it meant to be a priest.
You saw how he was of service to his fellow men.
You set out on a path, not knowing where it would
lead. You grew into the language of the faith and
into the various forms of service within the Church.
With the passing of time your image of the priest
has probably changed. You came to see more and
more clearly what a priest is and what he needs
to be in our time. You have gained a deeper
insight into the meaning of vocation.

St Paul described his vocation in a particularly
apt and striking way when he said that he was
"captured" by Christ; that he stretched forward
for what lay before him and left the past behind.
He runs, like a competitor in a race, to gain the

prize of his vocation. His vocation comes from above; it is from God; it is effected through Jesus Christ (*Phil 3:12-14*). He is under a unique constraint; he *must* proclaim the Gospel; he *must* speak of it. Necessity is upon me: woe to me if I do not preach the Gospel (*1 Cor 9:16*).

The apostle also refers to the recipients of this vocation: Not the wise, not the powerful, not those of noble birth has God chosen and called, but those whom the world regards as foolish, to shame the wise, those whom the world regards as weak, to shame the strong (*1 Cor 1:26-28*). This is the unique logic of God's calling. None of those called will be able to boast of his own achievements. God alone gives both the word and the power to proclaim it.

Neither does the apostle hide the consequences of such a vocation. He carries the treasure of the Gospel in a fragile, earthen vessel. He is afflicted in every way, but not crushed; he is perplexed but not driven to despair, persecuted but not forsaken, struck down but not destroyed. He always carries in his body the death of Jesus, so that the life of Jesus may shine forth bodily in him (*2 Cor 4:7-10*).

Only a man who had responded to his vocation with every fibre of his being could make such a breathtaking confession. But what he says is true, or can be true, for everyone who is called. Vocation to the Gospel is also a vocation to the Cross of Christ. All who respond to the call need to remember that. The man who proclaims the Gospel experiences in himself the prolongation of the passion and death of Jesus. A follower of Jesus cannot avoid confrontation with the power of evil. Only through this suffering can the change take place which manifests the new life of Jesus. Only the priest who has shared Christ's sufferings can speak convincingly of Christ's resurrection. Here again is an example of God's unique logic.

Our society differs from that of St Paul's time in that external persecution is rare. Yet, the priest of today can still suffer deeply. Some individuals, some groups, take little notice of him; his particular office and service are regarded as superfluous; there are those who look on him as a species of pious fool. And we must not ignore the fact that there can be real hatred and enmity against the servant of the Church. I am sure that you are prepared for this and have no illusions.

I want to refer to another cross, one you may have little experience of. It does not come from those outside the Church, but from those within, from the faithful themselves. I often think that this is a far harder cross to bear. It can happen that they range themselves into opposing groups; one group thinks you too conservative and resists you, while their opposite numbers regard you as an innovator and refuse to cooperate with you. There are others who raise doubts about the priesthood; they make you uncertain and cause you to doubt. None of these groups will listen to the others, and you find yourself unable to bring about a reconciliation. Again, you may be misunderstood by your superiors; perhaps you make a mistake and fail to set matters right with them. In the Church at present it seems to me that we ourselves are our heaviest cross; but that, too, can be a redemptive cross, so long as we are prepared to accept it and do not despair, getting up each time we fall under its weight. Giving up marriage and a family may be another hard cross for you, but I will write of that again. In all these trials we have St Paul's apt words: "I can do all things in him who strengthens me"; or, in St Augustine's variation: "Give what you command, and then command what you will." It may be that there cannot be *aggiornamento* in the Church without the suffering and cross-bearing of those called to be her servants.

In his *Confessions*, Augustine gives a moving account of the long path of his vocation, with its many painful detours. Moved by greed, he had sold his oratorical skills in the market of rhetoric. His head had been turned with the excitement of novelty; he was filled with the pride of life and the glamour of rhetoric. But at the same time he was overcome by boredom with his life and set out on the long, hard search for his vocation. Recalling that time, he says: "I bore about with me a shattered and bleeding soul, a soul impatient of being borne by me, yet where to repose it I found not" (*Confessions, IV*, 7).

It is a slow vocation. He feels himself spurred

25

on by "inner goads", until it becomes unbearable to exist without a glimpse of God and certainty about him. Augustine has to correct many errors in his belief and in his manner of life. He is shaken to the marrow on reading "the least of the apostles". The Greek academy cannot bring him fulfilment; only in faith in Christ does he realise that. For a long time he hesitates, wanting to seize his opportunity, being thrown back, turning in flight. Finally he acts — that is the grace of God. He is liberated and experiences "a quiet exultation". God pierces his heart with his Word: "I was at the mercy of the waves, and you were at the helm" (*Confessions, VI, 5*).

God's call is always different, unique. A person can abandon his vocation. He can sell it for a mess of potage. He can take risks with it or let it wither away. There are many ways in which this can happen without one realising it and it is a particularly dangerous possibility today; that is why a vocation to the Gospel must be continually developed and deepened. To take a vocation for granted — and that is all too easy — is to put it in jeopardy. On the other hand it can be endangered by an exaggerated activism. Like human love, a vocation must be cherished and there must be a response. Without this mutual affinity both love and vocation easily fade away. Perhaps the accommodating tendency of our theology inclines us to underestimate this danger.

A vocation is brought to fruition by being continually rooted in faith and by a constant deepening of one's spiritual life. You are forever concerned with the word of God: you catechise the children, you preach, you give talks or conduct Bible study. It is very easy to become "used to" the word of God. You have studied exegesis and you imagine that you know a lot about it. Without noticing it, you tend to act as if the word of God were under *your* control. You know it by heart. Perhaps one day it will mean nothing more to you than a string of commonplaces. It will have lost its power. It will slip like sand through your fingers. You will have lost your sense of wonder at the message.

You see where familiarity can lead. What can you do to counteract it? I think you must read the holy Scriptures regularly. You must read them with the simple, childlike eyes of faith. You must relate what you read to your life, leave yourself open to it. And you will have to leave your exegesis aside, because although it is good it can corrupt your "eye of faith" as you approach the word of God. For what you read there springs from disclosures in faith — God revealing himself to the authors of revelation. Behind every text there stands, not theories, but a meeting with the living God, and each text is intended to lead you to your own personal encounter with him.

If you neglect this personal encounter with the word of God, with God himself, or if you imagine that one such encounter is sufficient for your entire life, you will be ineffectual as a proclaimer of the word — even if, to all appearances, you are a success. A single encounter is not enough; just as with love, a single avowal is not enough. Hence, if you lose your sense of wonder at the word of God, you must take great pains to regain it; otherwise, those who hear you will not be gripped by the word. There is no simple recipe for re-capturing a lost sense of wonder: that is a matter of grace. But if you begin by marvelling first of all at ordinary things in human life, in your own life, and then consider how much of that is due to the Gospel, you will be astonished at what the Gospel means to you. Perhaps you, like Augustine, will experience a "quiet exultation" welling up within you.

As you are aware, the recitation of the breviary also promotes a regular encounter with the word of God and with God himself. Obviously it cannot succeed if it is done in a hurry. It needs time. It needs quiet. In our experience it was better to consider a few texts and pray them meditatively than to rush through many texts superficially. This insight, however, though good in itself, can become dangerous if taken to extremes; for the texts can get shorter and shorter until practically nothing is left. Or, if it is a "free selection", one easily tends to select only those texts which "say something to me", neglecting many others. Your proclamation then becomes one-sided; whereas the priest's task is to minister the Gospel in its entirety.

The recitation of the breviary is the fruit of the Church's age-old experience of faith and preaching and it is fitting that the entire Scripture should be read in a regular manner. In exceptional cases a man may be right in declaring that his life is "breviary enough"; but if this were to become the rule, there would be a danger of losing altogether the encounter with the word of God; I urge you not to underestimate that danger.

Meditation is another way of being rooted in faith. I hear that you young priests of today have a high regard for regular meditation; that is a hopeful sign. In silence the word crystallises. In silence you are present to yourself, taking in again what you have given out. In silence encounter with the word of God takes place. In silence you gather strength for renewed speech and renewed activity. The man who has no regular pattern of quiet will soon have nothing to say. Throughout his ministry Jesus always sought quiet, he sought conversation with his Father. Take no notice of those who decry meditation and noisily demand "action". What do they achieve?

Meditation is by no means opposed to activity but leads directly to it; it is a preparation-in-faith for activity and keeps us from rushing headlong and thoughtlessly into action. Our tendency to go to one extreme or the other is extraordinary! It was fine to have rediscovered Christian action, but that is no reason to downgrade meditation. To devalue all spiritual, interior life is a complete mistake. The inner life of faith is what the priest, the proclaimer of the Gospel, most urgently needs, especially today. He needs this continual encounter with the word of God if his own words are not to be utterly hollow and empty. At present there is a rediscovery of the interior life, especially among young people. It is indispensable if faith is to live.

The same is true of prayer, understood as the totality of linguistic acts of faith: these may be acts of wonder, thanks, petition, entreaty, or expressions of joy, exultation, confidence, love, praise — even of complaint; all of these are acts characteristic of human persons. Prayer is the form of our personal relationship with God; it is the unfolding, the growth, of faith into maturity. Prayer is the answer to God's call, to one's vocation. Of course our whole lives can be prayer but, if faith is no longer expressed in acts like those just mentioned, "making one's life a prayer" can become no more than a slogan. Prayer requires regularity; there are no grounds for questioning this fundamental insight of the Church.

By difficulties in prayer I mean chiefly the problem of the language we use in prayer. As yet we hardly have at our disposal a prayer-language suited to the world we live in; but a strong faith will create its own language. The Church today has great need of confident, whole-hearted prayer. In another letter I will explain why the Church has such need of the kind of priestly spirituality you are searching for. In your search, you will iend,

we see things differently I am glad that
ill willing to write to me. Here is a
hich concerns you as much as it does
er the service of the Gospel *requires* a
way of life. Many say that all Christians
to serve the Gospel and that therefore
lual Christian's way of life is a secondary
r they hold that the priest ought to live
ry midst of the secular world, sharing
f life of those to whom he preaches. Our
ociety in the Church is said to be contrary
n *mores*; and — a far more telling objec-
hat it is not in accord with the Gospel.
old that all Christians are priests and, as
ve equal rights and obligations.

time I favoured these views and listened
to those who advanced them; they were
at corresponded with my own wishes; for
nsure of myself and of my priesthood. Of
ave become more wary and have begun to
vhat I overlooked before. (This shows how
one needs to be regarding one's pet theories
inions.)

ing my study of linguistics I saw how a
te *life-form* goes together with a particular
age game". That a language is closely re-
o a life-form was one of the most important
eries of the late Wittgenstein. A life-form
s and sustains a language and gives it mean-
Vithout its appropriate life-form a language

need to follow the footsteps of Jesus, keeping the
eyes of faith fixed on him and aided by all your
biblical knowledge. You will take your bearings
from his security in God, his freedom from care,
his poverty.

All your life long you will strive to be a disciple;
in that striving each new circumstance will mean
that you must start from the beginning again. You
may be deflected from that path, so you will
need that unconditional faithfulness in which Jesus
lived, the confidence in God that informed his
actions and his preaching. His whole attitude will
determine, inspire and correct your own priestly
spirituality. That is a liberating way to live though
it does not mean avoidance of the Cross. If you
find that your path *does* appear to avoid the Cross,
you will have to ask yourself, "Am I on the right
track?"

Your other signpost will be the lives of the
saints, for they translated Christ's way of life into
the life of their own times. They form a bridge
between us and the Gospel way of life. Although
it is true that we cannot enter equally into the
world of every saint, there will be one or two who
will speak to you particularly clearly. Their witness, their writings will be a powerful support and
help in giving shape to your faith. The saints can
be like living companions on our way; for our
vocation is like theirs. Like them, we are called
to a *contemporary* holiness; weakness cannot
change the fact of a vocation. If every baptised

person may aspire to sainthood, how much more the priest?

Above all you will be ⟨...⟩ of what lies beyond, th⟨...⟩ a life with complete ha⟨...⟩

My dear fr⟨...⟩
Though ⟨...⟩
you are st⟨...⟩
question w⟨...⟩
me: wheth⟨...⟩
particular ⟨...⟩
are called ⟨...⟩
the individ⟨...⟩
matter. O⟨...⟩
in the ve⟨...⟩
the way ⟨...⟩
two-tier s⟨...⟩
to moder⟨...⟩
tion — th⟨...⟩
We are ⟨...⟩
such, ha⟨...⟩
For a ⟨...⟩
readily ⟨...⟩
ideas th⟨...⟩
I was u⟨...⟩
late I h⟨...⟩
notice ⟨...⟩
carefull⟨...⟩
and op⟨...⟩
Dur⟨...⟩
concre⟨...⟩
"langu⟨...⟩
lated ⟨...⟩
discov⟨...⟩
create⟨...⟩
ing. ⟨...⟩

dies out. Now, that applies particularly to the language of faith, behind which stands the life-form, the life of faith. The latter is founded on the linguistic acts of faith and the realisation and shaping of a personal relationship with God.

You may say: but this form of the life of faith is demanded of every Christian. It is precisely at this point that we resume the argument posed in the first lines of this letter. There *are* particular forms of response to the Gospel which are *not* required of every Christian. Think of the Evangelical Counsels; if they were lost, a fundamental expression of the Gospel would cease to exist. Or recall those demands made by Jesus to which we Christians are unable to respond in full. Yet the person who stakes his life completely and exclusively on Christ's word, accepts these demands on his life and *lives* them. There is much truth in the saying, "All the baptised are equal", but it is dangerous when isolated from its context; it levels down different life-forms and can stifle authentic expressions of Christian faith. I regret how slow I was to realise that.

The language of faith — to take one aspect only — shows that a specifically priestly form of life is both justified and necessary. Those who live this particular form are directed by the "disclosure situations" of faith, so that they may lead others to experience these disclosures, which are nothing other than encounters with God. Language would be a poor thing indeed if it used nothing but

35

linguistic symbols; it uses not only these but also non-linguistic symbols. The priesthood is one of these. It is a living sign of faith and of the reality of God; it is a sign of the Cross of Christ and also of his Resurrection.

Of course the life of every Christian is a sign of faith, but is the ordinary, everyday Christian life able to exhibit fully all the signs of faith, especially the more radical ones? That is a question we must ask ourselves. Without the priestly form of life, faith, I fear, would lose a fundamental dimension. The man who proclaims faith shows it forth decisively in his own life through signs — the signs are sacrifice, unbounded confidence in God, and suffering. He stakes his life on God. That is saying a great deal and the reality does not always measure up to it; but it is the basic symbol of faith. The priestly life, therefore, as a life-form, has a language function in that it *speaks*, it proclaims. A merely verbal *kerygma* would be ineffectual, a fact you, as a priest, are well aware of.

It is thus understandable why the Church regards the priesthood as immensely important. There was a time when I thought it did not matter and was constantly suggesting improvements. That time is past. I have acquired a reverence for a life-form, a language that has worn well — resulting as it does from the experience of life and faith of many centuries — crystallised in priestly ordination and the theology of the priesthood. The priestly life has to be rendered intelligible to each age, but it must keep intact the fundamental signs of faith. I am not at all sure that such is the case with all the reforms suggested today. I have become cautious.

Celibacy is a clear sign of the priest's total dependence on God, but I will return to that in another letter. Further signs of this dependence can be read in the life of Jesus, his helpful, loving way with people, for instance; his attitude towards property and earthly goods; his calm and freedom from worry. Service, help, simply being-for-people, is fundamental to the priestly form of life; so is the acceptance of suffering, which has an intrinsic dynamic power; obedience, too, in the context of faith, may be a similar sign, a sign of readiness to subordinate oneself in the common service of the Gospel. But you will have considered these signs yourself.

By living a particular form of life, by your words, you sustain a "world of meaning" for many people. You are for them a bearer of faith's world of meaning. At your age I was not aware of what that meant for society and for people's lives. On the contrary I almost felt that, being a priest, I was socially inferior; no one could convince me otherwise. We can only appreciate what a world of meaning is when it begins to disintegrate. Sociologists and psychologists describe the consequences of this for individuals. Today we seem to be experiencing a crisis of meaning, an anguished loss of the meaning of life.

As a priest you are now helping to maintain a world of meaning, although this function of yours is scarcely recognised by society. The only men modern society thinks worthy of recognition are scientists, politicians and businessmen. People take, or used to take, these men's philosophy of life for granted. I do not think that will continue for long, for people will become painfully aware of what they lack. Embittered by crisis after crisis, they will begin to seek some way out. That fact alone means that your life-form must not be surrendered. Faith is not, of course, the only world of meaning; our society today is pluralist. But our faith is by far the most comprehensive; only faith can comprehend death and give it a meaning.

At present we are still in enthusiastic pursuit of science and technical progress while we flee from the problem of life itself. However, that enthusiasm seems to be significantly on the wane. Soon we may be standing empty-handed, asking how we can come to terms with life; science neither concerns itself with this problem nor can it proffer any solution. Then perhaps you will see, with astonishing clarity, the necessity for your form of life — a form which expresses a world of meaning. Perhaps, then, that world of meaning will come into its own.

Until recently I never could understand why many of the faithful felt that their world collapsed when a priest had a grave fall or was laicised. Now I see the reason for this. For them the priest expressed a world of meaning; through his form of life he was a sign of transcendence, a living sign of God. Although the present generation has problems of faith and is being manipulated by the secularisers, people still seek for a sign of transcendence; it is evident that they are again looking for something greater than the merely empirical. Attitudes unlike those of the recent past are quite discernible: people are searching passionately for indications, as sociologists have observed. By your life as a priest you can be more than an "indication"; you can be a sign of that which they seek. It is a matter of interpreting their language.

To me the secularisers seem like deaf musicians. They build up a theory which cannot be demonstrated in any way, unaware of the evidence against them. It is a pity that the Church appears to be so vulnerable to them. People who have lost the meaning of life can be helped by you to follow traces of transcendence. At first you cautiously lead them towards the limits of the empirical world, while carefully preparing them for the transition. Great sensitivity is needed, not only to gauge the particular situation in which people are, but also to sense what they are looking for. It may seem strange, but the first thing they need from you is encouragement to go beyond, to transcend themselves. Personal help and social concern are secondary, though these make the fulfilment of the primary need possible. That is probably a repellent idea to modern ears, theologians included, but my experience of life has convinced me of its truth. You, a priest, are a sign of transcendence. A sign must be effective, and the effectiveness of your sign will be limited by your failures in love and humanity. Such failures may well be the greatest burden of your ministry.

To live such a life is difficult. Much depends upon community — community in faith, community with others in the same ministry. The faithful have a responsibility towards you and you towards them; but priests have also a responsibility towards one another. They need to cultivate sincere and deep dialogue among themselves on the level of faith as well as on the human level. Only in this way can doubts and the sense of insecurity be overcome. It needs to be a critical dialogue. In my time we had no such discussions and so were not in a position to protect one another against errors and pitfalls.

To be over-concerned with success is a great hindrance. We all hope that our undertakings will succeed and we probably need to succeed. But in the priesthood it is hard to judge real success, which is sometimes where it is least expected and most lacking where most noisily acclaimed. You will be more keenly aware of failure than of success. But it is in what appears outwardly as failure that God's logic is revealed. Servants of the Gospel are rarely successful — judging success by the world's standards; their seeming failures can be part of the life-giving Cross. Seen from the human viewpoint, Jesus himself was certainly not a successful man. The Gospel puts a large question-mark behind our idolising of success and achievement.

You and your fellow priests will try to shape your ministry anew, to form it so that it may be understood by your contemporaries. To do that you will need to go part of the way to meet the world, to go with its people. At the same time you will need to mark well the frontier of the "world" opposed to the Gospel and which, in biblical language, is *sin*. Today that frontier has become blurred and vague. We rushed enthusiastically towards the world, for we had felt stifled, we thought that the Church had treated the world in an over-negative manner. In our *bona fide* attempt to make good past mistakes and exaggerations, we failed to notice that we had embraced the world uncritically, without taking into account its manifold aspects. When at last our eyes were opened, for many it was too late.

So, go towards the world, for the people are there, but discern clearly where the frontier lies: it is where hate is, or exploitation, or deceit. Go with the people, but only as far as God's measuring-line allows you. You will suffer with them, almost endlessly; but you will not succumb, for your suffering will not be without meaning; it will be part of a great work which will succeed. You will laugh and enjoy yourself with your fellow men, weep and mourn with them, too. But above all you will be the frontier man, a sign of what lies beyond, that Beyond which can fill a life with complete happiness. You will experience some of this joy and reflect it to others.

I fear that what I have written about the greatness of your vocation is very lame. Words are too ordinary to convey its sublime meaning. I only wanted to tell you of what I myself was slow to realise. I hope you will give me your views on the matter when you reply.

Letter 4
Celibacy

Today, celibacy is unquestionably the sign of a life lived according to the Gospel; it is a sign of one who builds his life completely on God, peaceful, trusting, without the need to possess.

My dear friend,

As you have been expecting an answer from me on the question of celibacy, I am writing on that subject today.

I wrote about the priesthood being a sign of transcendence, a sign of a world of meaning. The promise to forego marriage is another sign, perhaps the most powerful one which the priesthood gives. It determines a form of life; it expresses the fact that a man has staked his whole life on God. It bears witness to the meaning of life, to a fervent faith, to a deep personal relationship with God. It gives immense force and cogency to the proclaimed word. No wonder that the Pope calls it "the pearl of great price".

Why, then, has celibacy become a controversial issue in recent times? There is no simple answer to that question. I can only tell you what happened to my fellow priests and myself. Our theological path has been described in an earlier letter. Many of us were oppressed by the thought that in our Church there seemed to be a hatred of the body, a Manichaeism. We felt that, because of this, our contemporaries were no longer able to believe simply and happily, that they regarded God as a rival to their lives and bodies. These ideas sank in, since we were set on finding a Gospel language intelligible to modern man.

We had no defence against self-criticism of this kind. Perhaps there were contrary arguments; if so, we did not understand them or, as time passed, we simply paid no heed to them. We saw that the faith of the Bible had overcome this hatred of the body, that it proclaimed the Resurrection of the Body, in other words, of the whole man. This was a joyful discovery for us and we regarded it as our task to do away with the Church's understanding of the role of the body; then a new start could be made in inviting people to share the Good News.

Obviously, in this context, little thought was given to the sign-value of celibacy. It was criticised from many angles; we began to hope that the Council would alter this particular sign and we listened eagerly to those who seemed to prophesy just that. Looking back now, I wonder did those who thus raised our hopes act responsibly? In any case we felt sure that the Council, having allowed the Eucharistic words of Consecration to be in the vernacular, would soon be in a position to abrogate priestly celibacy and would actually do so.

The Council made no decision, and we proceeded to the priesthood, some of us *in spite of* the lack of a favourable decision from Rome. It was a time of agonised wrestling with the problem. Our vocation to the ministry of the Gospel was so clear that no other possibility presented itself. We accepted celibacy as a sign of the Cross of Jesus, but, unfortunately, we had not filled out that sign with sufficient meaning; we had not fully identified ourselves with it. Perhaps it is in this respect that we were different from other generations of priests. And all the time we clung to the tiny hope that

the Church would come to a favourable decision—
a decision coinciding with our hopes — in the near
future.

So it was that for many of us celibacy was like
a "foreign body" in our lives. We had not totally
accepted it and that soon had consequences, for
we did not see its positive function. We heard it
spoken of as an obstacle to the proclamation of
the Gospel; we heard the priesthood described as
an unfulfilled life, a life incapable of manifesting
the Good News. So we looked for human fulfilment, considering that we had a "right" to it. The
next step was to take back the promise we had
given, to surrender the sign. After all, we told
ourselves, we had been called to the proclamation
of the Gospel; surely the Church would not "drop"
us.

I will not burden you with the intense inner
crises and torments of soul we endured. I only
want to give you some idea of the consequences
of false assumptions and expectations, and to keep
you from making similar mistakes. There were,
of course, many reasons why we failed to fully
integrate the sign of celibacy into our lives and
ministry. Among these were the confusing pressures and exploitation of modern advertising, the
exaggerated value placed on human sexuality, the
new cult of the body, the commercialisation of
sex, the constant betrayal of what is deepest in
man, and so on.

As I have said, it was late in the day before we

saw through all this, and some of us did not see even then. Fundamentally unsettled as we were, it was nevertheless our genuine desire to eliminate the traces of Manichaeism we saw in the Church. And we were not always aware of the issues being fought out around us, or of how we ourselves were being used as pawns in that struggle. One must regard the modern, more relaxed attitude towards the body and sexuality as a considerable gain; but the price paid for this was high and we can only hope that what has been lost in the process will yet be recovered. The Church's depreciation of the body has practically gone. A firm stand against the new cult of the body and of sex is now a more urgent need.

At present — and you may be surprised to hear this from me — the sign of celibacy which you bear is not only valid but positively essential and vital. One reason for this arises from the Gospel form of life, another stems from the world of our time and modern life. If I had realised this earlier, I would probably have taken a different path. It is true that Christ did not *oblige* those who were to be ministers of his word to accept celibacy, but he did commend it. Today, celibacy is unquestionably the sign of a life lived according to the Gospel; it is a sign of one who builds his life completely on God, peaceful, trusting, without the need to possess.

I believe that now this sign of celibacy can become deeply rooted again. In recent times the

Church has decided conclusively on the matter and that decision, however painful for many of us, seems to express the very essence of the matter. In this situation we need to learn to put the good of the Church before our own desires. With all my heart I wish that you may succeed in developing an untroubled relationship with the sign of celibacy, integrating it completely into your life. To achieve that, you will need to evaluate all things in life correctly and to develop a calm attitude towards Eros and sexuality — not depreciation, but a right proportion between body, soul and spirit.

Your freely chosen celibacy would not be an intelligible sign if seen in isolation. It needs to be manifested in its connection with other Gospel signs. This entails a detached attitude towards possessions; the renunciation of success and achievement; actual service, love and assistance; and occasionally the giving up of one's rights, of one's own wishes. All these support and help to interpret the celibacy-sign and point to the reality of God.

You are aware that you are holding on through a difficult time in the Church; you also need to remind yourself that you are helping to establish a new expression for a sign which many have come to regard with suspicion. It is not by words that you will convince them, but by your life. By combining a life-affirming and body-affirming attitude with a full commitment to the sign of celibacy, you will render that sign most clearly intelligible.

You will probably encounter spiritual problems on the way, but these can be solved by an ever deepening relationship with God.

In the working out of this priestly sign, many mistakes have been made, there have been many failures in charity. The arguments, because of the nature of the case, could not be other than highly emotional. But now verbal argument seems to have died down. What we need now is the argument of life, giving reality to the Church's decision. Those who recommended abandoning celibacy have forgotten that if such a powerful sign were given up it would need to be replaced by an equally powerful one. They have thus laid themselves open to the charge of wanting an easy, merely worldly life, of turning away from the Cross of Jesus. The discussion can proceed no further until they produce, and attempt to live, other signs of transcendence. Personally I doubt whether there is any equivalent sign. If our time were rich in transcendence one might find such a sign, but that is not the case, so the sign of celibacy is now more relevant than ever. We cannot choose the time in which our life-span is set, the time in which we live and are ministers of the Gospel. The very time we live in may be for us a cross.

So you should not have any reservations about your celibacy. Give it life and shape. Those around you who find it hard to talk about God will take notice of the sign. It may make them stop and reflect on their own lives; it may help them to see that there is more to life than what is empirical. You will probably never know in this life for whose sake you bear that sign. Sometimes you will be a sign of contradiction but on the whole you will be a sign revealing God, a pointer drawing attention to him. It will involve you in suffering, bringing you closer to Christ and enabling you to share in the transforming power of his Cross.

The modern cult of Eros and its subtle forms of exploitation can be foiled by exhibiting an alternative way of life and by preserving a sense of humour. But if you wish to be understood avoid fanaticism. You will need the calmness which comes from a faith that says: "I do not need to have everything men think valuable and important. I must serve my fellow men and this can only be done by self-denial and the free acceptance of the cross. God will give me the strength to do what he requires of me." Such an attitude would liberate many people today.

Clerical clothes were also the sign of a life-form; they still can be this sign. We often imagine that people do not understand, and hence become unsure of ourselves. I remember, when we were preparing for ordination, many of us regarded the priest's attire as a cramping constraint; we had quite an inferiority complex about it. Rules and custom have been relaxed since then, which is a good thing. But it would be a pity if a priest's clothes bore no sign of his priesthood; his dress is part of the language of his life-form, a non-verbal sign of service and of the Gospel. Try and retain this sign in some form.

Regarding my own situation, I have sought and found human fulfilment. In doing so I have forfeited my service as a priest and, to a large extent, my ministry of the Gospel. I have little opportunity now to preach the Gospel. At the same time my vocation to the Gospel has not diminished; rather, it has matured and I have gained a new awareness of it. You can imagine how hard my position is: I cannot and will not stifle that inner call, and yet I can no longer follow it. St Paul says: "I am constrained; woe to me if I do not preach the Gospel." Everyone who has a vocation knows this feeling. It is a cross and like all crosses has the power to transform.

Those of us who have taken this decision have lost our standing in the Church. We are accused of breaking a promise, of running away from the Cross of Jesus, of failing in faith, of injuring the Church. We cannot attempt a defence in words, but only by a form of life. Even if our decision were subjectively correct it remains true that, in the context of the Church, it was the gravest error possible. And it was a transgression against love of the community, against our brother priests, against you who were to come after us. But even in a situation of disobedience there remains the hope of the pardoned sinner; it is possible to be borne up and carried by the grace of God. Such is his unfathomable way.

So I ask you to understand our position, even if you must condemn us. Do not utterly break off communication with us. For we share your vocation and would like to follow it; we keep hoping that the Church may yet find another way for us. Today this is difficult, as the dispute over celibacy has not yet completely subsided. So our life goes on and our vocation will not have been in vain. Help to find and prepare a way for us that we, too, may follow our call. That was one of my reasons for beginning this correspondence with you; the other was to warn you of the pitfalls all around us today and into which I fell.

I would say to you, adapting the words of Bertolt Brecht: "But you, my brethren, when Christians have succeeded in understanding one another better, think of us kindly, remembering that we emerged from dark days." Our time in the Church began bright and promising and raised towering hopes; it became overcast and gloomy with insecurity and the loss of communication. We passed through that darkness but we did not emerge unscathed. Time has moved on. Many of us have learned in the darkness and would like to communicate that knowledge. Think of us and do not refuse the outstretched hand!

Letter 5
Dialogue and Criticism

Just as the one we love most can cause us most pain, so the Church can make us suffer; we share in her tribulations. Be prepared to shoulder that burden; it can be for you the promise of the resurrection.

My dear friend,

Thanks for giving me so much of your time. I would like to raise another important contemporary issue, i.e. dialogue and criticism in the Church. In virtue of your radical discipleship of Christ you are in a special way responsible for his Church. You can never be indifferent to what goes on in the Church, to the behaviour of your fellow Christians. In a particular situation you may find yourself obliged to speak a word of clarification or of criticism. On such occasions it is essential that what you say is understood in the sense you mean it to be understood.

Nowadays we have more than enough criticism and self-criticism in the Church; and I can imagine that you, more than others, find this trying. Criticism of the kind we hear seldom has the desired effect; it is hardly ever correctly understood; above all, it rarely serves to build up the Church. Instead it creates confusion and insecurity; it pulls down and destroys. To criticise is to engage in a verbal act which either succeeds or fails. This action follows certain determinate rules. If it fails it means that these fundamental rules are being violated. Often the critic merely propagates his own insecurity. Much of the present criticism of the Church arises from a theology which, increasingly, seems to have lost its heart and, in large measure, its head.

It is precisely the young who suffer because of the errors and aberrations they see within the

Church. They dream of an ideal Church and are intolerant of human weakness. They say what they think they see; they identify what seems to them to be wrong, and they are amazed to find that their criticism does not succeed, that they become voluble outsiders. They are forced into a role they themselves reject. As you know, I myself was very much involved in that kind of criticism. Again and again I was astonished to find my criticism ineffective, my real intention misunderstood. Since then I have given much thought to the rules of criticism and to the mistakes their transgression can cause.

Since we share in a common service of the Gospel, we — as Christians — are responsible for one another, and for the fulfilment of the Gospel in the world. So we should watch for aberrations and bring them to light. This is probably what St Paul refers to as "prophetic speech", and he invites all to desire it (*1 Cor 14:1*). But this prophecy is for *building up* the Church. If it does not do this it is not true prophetic speech, and that seems to exclude much of what claims to be modern "prophecy". Everything depends on how the criticism is expressed, in what spirit correction is offered. According to the linguistic analyst, J. L. Austin, it is the failures of a linguistic act which reveal the rules of that act.

I think that every critic has to begin with himself, his own defective religious attitudes, his own weakness. In this way he gains a correct and humane appreciation of the weaknesses of others. Again, he must engage in dialogue with the object of his criticism before giving his judgment, and he must maintain that dialogue right through. It should be a mutual investigation, with critic and criticised exploring together the possibility of a change in attitude. Perhaps the other party, not the critic, should initiate the dialogue. This would require much faith and human courage, but I do not think that the problem which besets us today can be solved in any other way.

If the critic is left to himself, if barriers are erected or dialogue broken off, he is driven further into his critical attitude, into a vicious circle from which he cannot escape by his own efforts. The only way to help him is to ask him what he is actually looking for. Even when his criticism is in error, it can be turned to good. By approaching him in this way a lot of constructive power can be set free. There is another rule: criticism is primarily a life-form. The critic's own life must be a convincing advertisement for his cause. That is the saints' way and it remains the only effective way.

I have learned from experience. I would hate to think of you being drawn into that whirlpool of destructive criticism which is useless even when well-meant. Today we have too much verbal criticism and too little criticism *by life*. Criticism through a life-form comes close to the Cross; the critic may accept that Cross in the same spirit as his own weaknesses. Without breaking the bond of charity he is able to offer criticism calmly and not without a touch of humour. Only such criticism can correct wrong attitudes and build up the Church. If you could develop that it would bring great joy to me.

Like others, I feel saddened that our efforts at criticism served only to bring about a "devaluation of language" in the Church. I aimed at drawing attention, in a pointed and exaggerated manner, to what I thought needed correction. I wanted to demonstrate the Church's residual hatred of the body. But that verbal action failed, and I did not succeed in my purpose. I have since realised that my way led into a dead-end. The criticism exerted by a life takes precedence over verbal criticism. Lived criticism is a living dialogue. One needs to be very careful with criticism and with the spoken word generally. As soon as the words have left your lips you have no more control over them; then they do what they please.

Your function in the Church includes that of the critic, critic of yourself and of your fellow Christians. No one can absolve you from that task. We who are baptised are still sinners; we have an obligation to indicate to one another our sins and our failings. This, if it is to be successful, requires great effort and much prayer. You also face the world as its critic, for you do not share its deeds or its aims, you live a different life-form. It is your duty to speak whether the times be propitious or not, and to speak in a way that will be understood. You will bear with people and not judge them. You will strive to find other ways for them. The Gospel is not of this world; its logic differs from human logic. That is an implied criticism and if you take it seriously, it will mean suffering.

Your primary service is to the Church, the Church as it is today in all its tangible expressions. That often means ministering to people whose faith has become unsteady. Your main objective must be slowly to dissipate this insecurity and to prepare the way for faith to take deep root again. But how? First I think you must strive for a firm basis for your own faith. You need to be clear in your own mind about the causes, the failures, which led to the present uncertainty. Theological vanity and presumption played their part in it; so did basic mistakes in the process of criticism, lack of charity and breakdown in dialogue. Your task will be to show, carefully, how these errors arose and how they can be corrected.

Dialogue — the art, or the grace of dialogue — will prove your greatest help. It is disheartening to find that often Christians cannot continue to talk with one another, that sometimes whole groups entrench themselves and form enclaves holding one-sided views, that there is no longer any communication between them. You must act as the mediator. The most important thing to do at this stage is to re-create an atmosphere of confidence; then, freed from fear, people can concen-

trate on the Gospel common to all. To re-establish
this confidence it must first be evident in your own
life. That will involve being very careful when
preaching, teaching or conversing — not to create
further uncertainty. Remember that theological
theories and theses are not the *kerygma*!

We need to re-establish the lapsed communi-
cations between Christians; to do this you will
probably have to agonise over each individual,
just as Paul in Thessalonika had first to seek for
individuals and win them for Christ one by one.
Internal dialogue within the Church is even more
pressing than communication with those outside;
but this must not be mere discussion *about* the
Gospel — there is always the danger of talking
the subject to death — but a common undertaking
to recover the fundamental, verbal acts of faith.

Once you have succeeded in reawakening a
sense of wonder in the faithful at the greatness of
the Gospel, you will find that cross-frontier communication becomes easier; and, provided that
you yourself have this sense of wonder, you can
be a herald of faith. For that is your task — proclamation, not discussion. There is a fundamental
difference between them; proclamation consists of
non-descriptive verbal acts, discussion of descriptive argument. You should aim at arousing verbal
acts of thanksgiving to the God who is the cause
and object of our wonder. Through dialogue across
the boundary lines people can be led on towards
the areas conducive to faith, towards disclosure-

situations. You should try to stimulate verbal acts of prayer, supplication, yearning, joy and praise. Success will depend on your being possessed, to the depths of your being, by the word of faith and by the way your whole life-form expresses that. Under these conditions faith takes root; after that, barriers, real or imaginary, present no problem.

The Church, the parish where you serve, will be a joy to you. You will experience the sense of fulfilment at being needed, used. You will share the gladness of those who have been set free by a new or rediscovered faith; on the other hand you will also share the misery of those whose faith has trickled away completely. The Church herself will be a source of joy, also of pain, to you; just as the one we love most can cause us most pain, so the Church can make us suffer; we share in her tribulations. Be prepared to shoulder that burden; it can be for you the promise of the resurrection.

Suffering may come from without, from misunderstanding, as when people refuse to hear what you are bound to say. It may come from your life-form, from your renunciation of family, of human love and affection. This may sometimes shake the very roots of your being; your faith may be attacked; you may experience times of dryness and darkness, you may seem to have lost serenity of soul. But all this can be part and parcel of your life with God, of his dealings with you. In a more marked way than others you have committed yourself to the glorious adventure of faith, an adventure you embark upon on behalf of many others, for all who are concerned to know the meaning of their lives.

You can be quite relaxed in dealings with reductionists and merely verbal critics, even if they deny the validity of your life-form, provided that your own faith and interior life have deep roots. This will give you a light and generous touch. Never refuse to engage in dialogue, but avoid fanaticism. Be receptive to new arguments, provided that they are reinforced by a lived faith. You need not be particularly impressed by those intent on reforming the "structures", knowing that your ministry is to men, not structures, and the first task is to change men; that done, Church structures will take care of themselves. In all this my wish is that you may possess that calmness which befits the minister of the Gospel and which we, in our time, did not possess.

You will hear many rallying cries in the Church, even on occasion use them yourself. But if you are trying to live from the resources contained in the Gospel you will not let yourself be carried away by these slogans which are often simply the signs of fear and lack of confidence. Your firmness must be based on the Gospel. Then there is all the talk of "crisis" in the Church. See the facts as they are, but do not listen to those who exaggerate and complain. Crisis always accompanies a period of change and today there are clear indications that the change — and it began long ago — is a positive one. People outside the Church who live in affluence and superfluity are asking for a meaning to their lives, for they see that the values they once accepted have vanished and that an "existential vacuum" has replaced them.

In actual fact this is the Church's opportunity to provide a new framework of meaning. To do that she must stand by the entire content of the faith, there must be no watering down. She needs to be a questioning Church, but disintegration and loss of identity could rob her of her power to convince. Much is being done, following a period of radical criticism, to recover and rediscover a sense of identity. The fruits of criticism must, of course, be incorporated into this newly-acquired identity.

A world of meaning is not something that stands alone. It cannot survive apart from a worked-out, institutional embodiment; and the Gospel's framework of meaning stands or falls with the institutional embodiment found in the Church. We have almost accustomed ourselves to belittle the bearers of ecclesiastical office, setting up prophets and charismatics in opposition to them. It should be remembered that the very functioning of an institution is by no means automatic and self-explanatory and that there can be — and in fact are — not a few prophets and charismatics among those who bear office.

You, too, bear office in the Church; you, too, sustain that world of meaning. I have tried to show you how I see it all and to indicate a number of false presuppositions and assumptions. We greatly need you to live your particular form of life; it accompanies the word you preach and, indeed, prepares the way for it. We need that word, for it has power to change men, to change the world. We all need to be strengthened in faith. I would be happy to think that through this correspondence I had contributed a little towards strengthening you in your vocation.